WILD DOGS

Published by Creative Education, 123 South Broad Street, Mankato, Minnesota 56001

Copyright © 1996 by Wildlife Education, Ltd. Copyright 1996 hardbound edition by
Creative Education. All rights reserved. No part of this book may be reproduced in any form
without written permission from the publisher. Printed in the United States.

Printed by permission of Wildlife Education, Ltd.

Library of Congress Cataloging-in-Publication Data

Biel, Timothy L.
Wild dogs / written by Timothy Levi Biel.
p. cm. — (Zoobooks)
Includes index.
Summary: Discusses the habits and behavior of wild dogs, including the gray wolf,
jackal, dingo, fennec, bat-eared fox, and coyote.
ISBN 0-88682-780-9
1. Wild dogs—Juvenile literature. [1. Wild dogs.] I. Title. II. Series: Zoo books
(Mankato, Minn.)
QL737.C22B52   1996
599.74'442—dc20   95-45320   CIP AC

WILD DOGS

Creative Education

Art Credits

All paintings: Mark Hallett, assisted by Walter Stuart

Photographic Credits

Front Cover: Wayne Lynch (*DRK Photo*)

Pages Six and Seven: Stephen Krasemann (*DRK Photo*)

Page Ten: Tom McHugh (*Photo Researchers*)

Page Eleven: Top Left, Nadine Orabona (*Tom Stack & Associates*); **Top Right,** Leonard Lee Rue; **Bottom,** Jen & Des Bartlett (*Bruce Coleman, Ltd.*)

Pages Fourteen and Fifteen: Larry Brock (*Tom Stack & Associates*)

Page Sixteen: Top, Comstock; **Bottom,** Cyr Color Photo

Page Seventeen: Kenneth Fink (*Ardea London*)

Page Eighteen: Jen & Des Bartlett (*Survival Anglia*)

Page Nineteen: Gary Milburn (*Tom Stack & Associates*)

Page Twenty-One: Top, Russ Kinne (*Photo Researchers*); **Middle,** Jerry Cooke (*Photo Researchers*); **Bottom,** Richard Hutchings (*Photo Researchers*)

Pages Twenty-Two and Twenty-Three: Tom and Pat Leeson (*Photo Researchers*)

Our Thanks To: Veronica Tagland; Michaele Robinson (*San Diego Zoo Library*); Ed Hamilton (*San Diego Bionomics*); Dr. Dickson Phiri (*Mesa College*); Marvin Jones (*San Diego Zoo*); Michael Cassem; Stephen Kuntz (*Wolf Haven, Tenino, Washington*); Jack Laufer (*Wolf Haven*)

Cover Photo: Coyote

Contents

Wild dogs are beautiful, intelligent animals that deserve our admiration. But people often dislike and fear them. For example, people have heard many fairy tales that portray wolves as big, bad monsters lurking in the woods and waiting to attack. Or they may have heard stories of coyotes and other wild dogs killing such domestic animals as cows, sheep, chickens, and even pet dogs and cats.

These stories do not paint a fair picture. It is true that wild dogs are hunters. But they do not kill nearly as many domestic animals as people think. They kill rats, mice, and other animals that destroy farmers' crops, so most of their hunting is actually helpful to humans.

As for attacks on people, there has never been a proven case of a wolf or any other wild dog killing a human being. People, on the other hand, have been attacking and killing wild dogs for hundreds of years. Wild dogs really have more reason to fear us than we have to fear them.

It's curious that many people who hate wild dogs *love* domestic dogs. In fact, many of the things people like best about domestic dogs come from their wild ancestors. For example, most wild dogs are every bit as intelligent and loyal as domestic dogs.

This helps them to be excellent, devoted parents. Females usually give birth to a litter, or group, of two to ten pups each year. Both parents care for them until they are fully grown. Generally, only one or two pups from each litter survive beyond the first year. These may live to be 12 or 13 years old. In zoos, wild dogs often live more than 20 years.

There are many different kinds of wild dogs in the world. The largest is the gray wolf. A big male may weigh more than 150 pounds (68 kilograms) and stand 3 feet tall at the shoulders (91 centimeters). The smallest wild dog in the world is the *fennec*. This tiny fox from northern Africa may stand only 1 foot high at the shoulders (30 centimeters) and weigh less than 5 pounds (2.3 kilograms). Turn the page to find the gray wolf and the fennec.

Wolves may travel as many as 35 miles a day (56 kilometers), covering all types of terrain—hills, valleys, forests. Timber wolves like these once lived all across North America. Now they live in wilderness areas where there are few people.

How many kinds of wild dogs do you think there are? Most people can only think of three or four, but altogether there are about 35 different species in this family. Of these, 15 are shown here.

The very first wild dogs lived in North America. These dogs were excellent hunters, and they adapted quickly to new climates and surroundings. Over thousands of years, they spread to every continent except Antarctica. Their bodies gradually developed in different ways to survive in different parts of the world. These changes led to the different species of wild dogs that exist today.

ARCTIC FOX
Alopex lagopus

COYOTE
Canis latrans

FENNEC
Vulpes zerda

GRAY FOX
Urocyon cinereoargenteus

RED WOLF
Canis rufus

MANED WOLF
Chrysocyon brachyurus

BUSH DOG
Speothos venaticus

8

GRAY WOLF
Canis lupus

RED FOX
Vulpes vulpes

RACCOON DOG
Nyctereutes procyonoides

BLACK-BACKED JACKAL
Canis mesomelas

DHOLE
Cuon alpinus

AFRICAN WILD DOG
Lycaon pictus

BAT-EARED FOX
Otocyon megalotis

DINGO
Canis lupus familiaris dingo

Sun-baked deserts and frozen tundra are *both* good homes for wild dogs. As a group, wild dogs have adapted to more different places in the world than any other group of predators. For example, wild dogs that live in grasslands may be tall so they can see over tall grass. A few wild dogs live where there is a lot of brush, so they have short legs for running through it. Some that live in forests are good tree climbers. And those that live along rivers are good swimmers.

No matter where they live, the main reason that wild dogs can survive in so many places is that they eat almost anything. If they can't find one kind of prey, they will hunt something else. And when meat is scarce, they eat plants and insects.

The fennec has huge ears for its size, and they help it stay cool in the Sahara Desert. Heat escapes quickly from such large, flat surfaces, and this helps cool the fox's whole body. The fennec is also an extremely good digger, so it can escape the heat by digging shallow burrows in the sand.

BUSH DOG

The bush dog of South America doesn't even look like a dog. But its short legs are perfectly suited for living near rivers and streams. Its broad paws make excellent paddles, so the bush dog can dive and swim under water. It uses these swimming skills for hunting, as shown at right.

Tiny ears help the Arctic fox survive in the severe cold. Since they do not expose much surface to the cold air, these ears do not lose much heat. The Arctic fox's woolly fur also helps it to stay warm, even when the temperature drops to minus 90 degrees Fahrenheit (minus 67 degrees Celsius)! When it is caught in a blizzard, this fox curls up in a tight ball and uses its bushy tail to cover its face.

Bush dogs often catch pacas and other large rodents in the water. When a paca is chased, it usually runs into the water to escape. The bush dogs take advantage of this by working in teams. One dog chases the paca into the water, while another one waits there for it.

You've seen *cats* up in trees, but have you ever seen a *dog* in a tree? Gray foxes live deep in the woods, and they are excellent tree climbers. They often climb trees to find shelter, and to watch for mice and other small prey that pass below.

The legs on this wild dog are so long that it appears to be walking on stilts! But these "stilts" help the maned wolf live in the grasslands of South America. They raise the wolf high enough to see prey over the top of the grass. And they make it easier for the wolf to run through the grass to catch its prey.

GRAY FOX

When meat is hard to find, many wild dogs survive on fruits and berries. This fox is standing on its hind legs so it can reach the ripest berries on the bush.

PATAGONIAN GRAY FOX

One of the best hunters among all wild dogs is the dhole, or Asian red dog. But sometimes even this excellent hunter must rely on a meal of wild rhubarb, as shown at right.

11

Wild dogs are runners. Unlike cats and other predators that *hide* and wait for prey to come to them, wild dogs *chase* their prey for long distances. They are not the fastest runners in the animal kingdom, but they have great endurance.

The coyote shown on these pages can reach a top speed of 40 miles per hour (64 kilometers per hour), and at slightly slower speeds, it can run for miles. So if it can stay close to its prey, it has a good chance of overtaking it.

Because wild dogs do not have big powerful jaws like cats do, they cannot kill large prey animals alone. It may take several of them to bring down a large animal. Their long, thin jaws are made for grabbing prey and hanging on to it. The long jaws also provide space for a large nose. This is one of the things that helps wild dogs sense food and danger, as you see below.

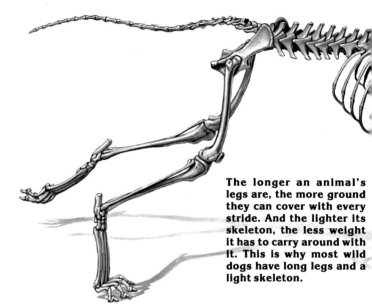

The longer an animal's legs are, the more ground they can cover with every stride. And the lighter its skeleton, the less weight it has to carry around with it. This is why most wild dogs have long legs and a light skeleton.

Wild dogs have large pointed ears that act like big scoops to catch lots of sound. They can hear sounds that are too faint for you to hear. And their ears are so sensitive, they can also hear sounds that are too *high-pitched* for human ears.

Even when it sleeps, a wild dog's ears stand straight up—so it can catch sounds made by other animals at all times. This helps the wild dog catch prey, and lets it know when danger is near.

A dog's nose can smell things that your nose can't. Like your nose, the inside of a dog's nose contains moist surfaces that "catch" smells in the air. As shown below, the wild dog's nose has about five times more surface area than yours does. So it can catch more smells from the air than you can. The nose itself is not five times larger than a human nose. For all the extra smelling surface to fit inside, it must be wrapped and folded many times.

SEE FOR YOURSELF how so much smelling surface can fit into a dog's nose. Cut out two pieces of paper, one about 5 times bigger than the other. Fold the smaller piece 3 times, as shown at right Ⓐ. This is like the surface area inside a human's nose. Now fold the larger piece about 10 times Ⓑ. This is like the surface area inside a dog's nose.

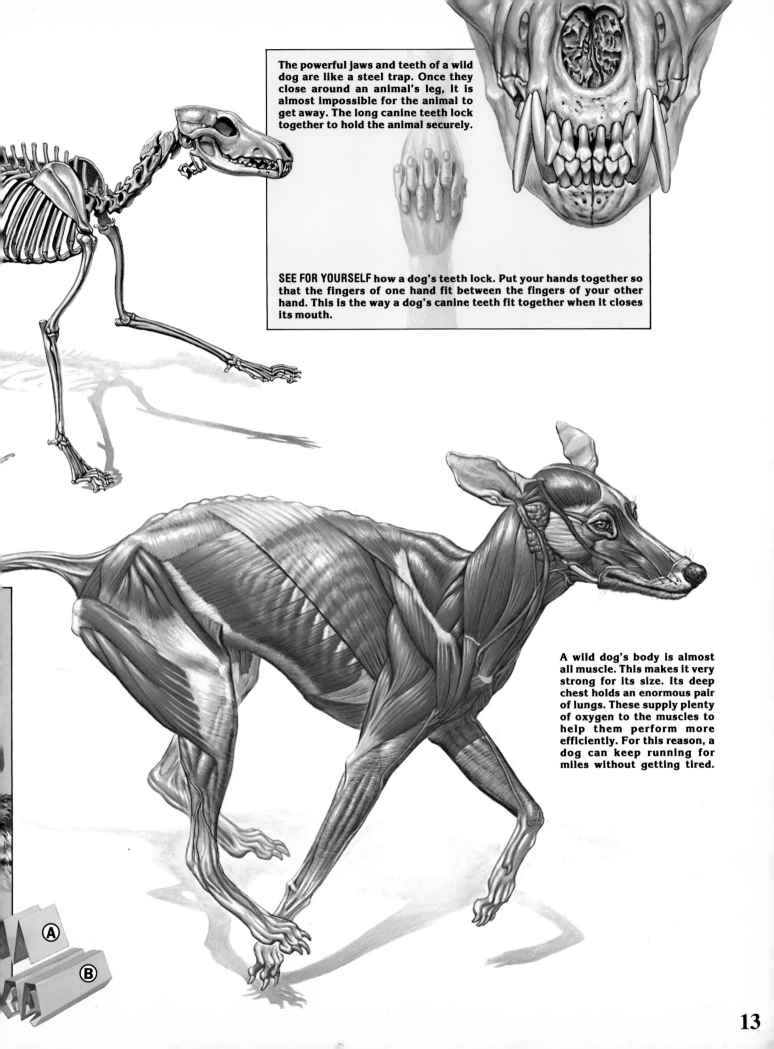

The powerful jaws and teeth of a wild dog are like a steel trap. Once they close around an animal's leg, it is almost impossible for the animal to get away. The long canine teeth lock together to hold the animal securely.

SEE FOR YOURSELF how a dog's teeth lock. Put your hands together so that the fingers of one hand fit between the fingers of your other hand. This is the way a dog's canine teeth fit together when it closes its mouth.

A wild dog's body is almost all muscle. This makes it very strong for its size. Its deep chest holds an enormous pair of lungs. These supply plenty of oxygen to the muscles to help them perform more efficiently. For this reason, a dog can keep running for miles without getting tired.

Ⓐ

Ⓑ

13

Like many wild dogs, the coyote is usually active at night, when it can hunt safely. You can often see coyotes in the early evening and morning, as they come to and from their nighttime activities.

14

Family is very important to most wild dogs. Male and female dogs often stay together for years, sometimes even for life. They raise their pups together, and in some of the larger species, the young may stay with their parents after they've grown up. In this way, they form large family groups known as *packs*.

In a pack of wild dogs, all the adults feed and care for all the young. This strengthens family ties and keeps the group together. The adults protect the pups from danger. When the pups grow older, they are taught to hunt with the pack.

Like human communities, packs of wild dogs must be well organized. They must have leaders to make decisions and settle arguments. They must have followers that know how to do certain jobs. And like people in a community, they must be able to help each other, as you see below.

When they are attacked, a family of wild dogs will fight as a group to protect one another. Below, a pair of black-backed jackals are working together to defend their young from a hyena. (A hyena is *not* a wild dog, as many people think.)

One way that wild dogs can help each other is by "talking" to one another. They can even do this over long distances. If a wolf is separated from its pack, it howls loudly until the other wolves hear it. Then they howl in reply, and the lone wolf follows the sound until it finds them.

In a human community, a single adult may take care of many children. The same is true in a pack of wild dogs. When a wolf pack goes off to hunt, for example, an older female wolf may be left behind to babysit.

One adult jackal may carry the pups to safety Ⓐ, while another tries to keep the hyena busy Ⓑ. When other pack members hear these jackals barking, they come running to the rescue Ⓒ.

Ⓒ

Wild dogs can "talk" without making a sound! They do this by using their bodies. For example, the leader of a group of Golden Jackals may push the other jackals around by swinging its hips at them. This is the leader's way of reminding the other jackals who is the boss.

Making faces is another way that wild dogs "talk" to one another. They have several different expressions that have different meanings. Can you guess what the two jackals at right are "saying?" Which of the two is angry, and which one is friendly? Check for the correct answers in the lower right corner of this page.

① ②

African wild dogs can be savage hunters. But with each other, these dogs are loyal, gentle, and loving. Male and female mates show their affection for each other by licking, nuzzling, or just lying close together.

AFRICAN WILD DOGS

ANSWER: Jackal ① is being friendly. Jackal ② is angry.

Wild dogs hunt in several different ways, depending on the size of their prey. A wolf, for example, may hunt alone when going after small prey like rabbits or squirrels. Or it may team up with two or three other wolves to hunt for deer. To go after a big moose, it may hunt with 10 or 15 other wolves. African wild dogs sometimes form packs of 60 or more in order to hunt big prey, like the zebra below.

When hunting together, all members of the pack must do their jobs correctly. They must follow their leader's directions, send and understand signals, and work together. On these pages, you will see some of the different ways that wild dogs hunt.

Most foxes hunt alone, which means that they must hunt for small prey. The Red Fox has a very effective way of catching mice. First, it listens and smells until it figures out exactly where the mouse is hiding. Then suddenly, it leaps high into the air ①.

With deadly accuracy, the fox lands right on top of the mouse and holds it to the ground with its front paws ②.

BLACK-BACKED JACKAL

Scavenging is one way that jackals and other wild dogs get food. This means cleaning meat from the bones of dead animals. People often think of scavengers as filthy animals. But they perform an important service in nature by cleaning up after other predators. Sometimes jackals must fight off other scavengers, like the vultures shown above.

There is no way that a single African wild dog could capture a large zebra. But by hunting together in packs, they can easily bring down huge prey. The first dogs to reach the zebra try to grab it and hang on until the others get there.

The bat-eared fox has some "special equipment" for hunting in a special way. It lives mainly on termites, and with its enormous ears, it can actually hear these tiny insects running through their underground tunnels!

BAT-EARED FOX

Dingos are the only wild dogs on the continent of Australia. Their ancestors were probably domestic dogs that came to Australia with the first humans who settled there. Dingos have since taken to the wild, where they have become very good at hunting in pairs for kangaroos. Over a short distance, a kangaroo is faster, but the dingos just stay close to it until it gets tired.

When hunting large animals, like caribou, a pack of wolves often uses a special strategy. First, the wolves separate a few of the caribou from the rest of the herd ①. Then they try to single out a young or weak individual. One of the wolves may try to startle it by barking ②.

The remaining pack members circle around to the other side of the chosen prey ③. When it is startled and bolts, the wolves quickly surround it.

19

People love dogs. In fact, people breed and keep more than *400 different kinds* of domestic dogs as pets. Most scientists believe that every one of these breeds is descended from the wolf. About 20,000 years ago, wolves probably became the first wild animals to be domesticated by humans.

Of course, there are no written records that tell us exactly when or how this happened. However, scientists have studied ancient relics and cave paintings to acquire an understanding of the way that wolves were domesticated. You can follow the steps in this process by starting with the picture below.

② Gradually, people realized that wild dogs could help them. With their superb senses, wolves could lead them to prey and warn them whenever danger was near. So they began to take young wolf pups from the wild and raise them by hand. Before long, there were enough pet wolves to provide a growing number of new puppies.

Wolves adjusted to people easily. They are extremely social animals that live in groups. They are used to working together and following leaders. Some wolves just began to accept humans as their leaders.

③

Over thousands of years, domestic dogs began to behave very differently. Instead of being trained to hunt, many dogs were trained to guard sheep and cattle from wolves and other predators.

④

As time went on, dogs changed even more. They looked different from their wild ancestors, and their behavior was almost entirely different. Some domestic dogs were raised just to look cute and be good companions.

⑤

①

Some wild dogs probably began to depend on humans thousands of years ago, when people lived as wandering hunters. Wolves may have followed the roaming bands of hunters so they could eat the scraps of food that people left behind. They slowly overcame their fear of humans and drew closer to their camps.

Today, people have pet dogs of almost every size and shape. There are dogs that are as big as a pony and other dogs that can fit in your hand.

⑥

We appreciate the loyalty and intelligence of domestic dogs. Some of them serve us faithfully like this *seeing-eye dog*, which guides its blind master. Unfortunately, many people are unable to appreciate the loyalty and intelligence of this dog's wild relatives, as you see at right.

People often blame wild dogs for things they don't do. Ranchers may think that coyotes kill thousands of their sheep and cattle. Many of these animals actually die from other causes, and the coyotes scavenge their remains. But people still blame them, and try to get rid of coyotes any way they can.

BOUNTY $10.00

Survival is difficult for many wild dogs in today's world. There was a time when wild dogs were so good at survival that they spread to almost every part of the world. But people have changed all that. Some of the wild dogs that once were most successful, now have the worst time living near humans.

Wolves are a good example of this. They once roamed over most of the world north of the Equator. As more and more people moved into places where wolves lived, they began to compete with these predators for game. Gradually, people built towns and cleared land for farms. They raised sheep and cattle in the wolves' old hunting grounds. As it became more difficult to find their natural prey, some wolves began to take domestic animals instead.

Wolves were such good hunters that people felt threatened by them. And this led to a showdown. But the wolves were no match for the rifles, traps, and poisons that people used against them. Soon their numbers dropped so low that wolves were no longer a threat to anyone.

Unfortunately, some people were slow to realize this. They went on hunting wolves until they became seriously endangered. Today, there are only a few thousand gray wolves left in the world. The red wolves that once lived throughout the southern United States can now be found only in zoos and wild animal preserves.

The same thing has been happening to other wild dogs around the world. Unless something is done to save them, African wild dogs, Asian dholes, and most species of wolves will soon be gone. These are all large species of wild dogs that hunt in packs. They need larger hunting territories and bigger prey than other wild dogs, and that is one reason they are having so much trouble.

Scientists have studied the needs of these animals, and they believe that with our help most of them can be saved. To do this, people must set aside large wilderness areas where packs of wild dogs can hunt their natural prey. But that won't be easy. Many people still feel threatened by them and would like to get rid of them. They must learn that wild dogs are no longer the serious threat they once were. And they must realize that these predators play an important role in nature. Wild dogs help make our world a more beautiful and more interesting place to live.

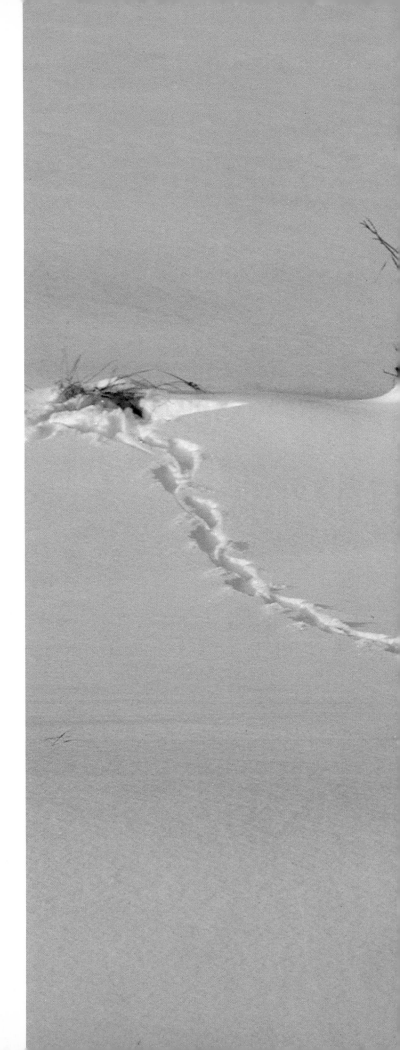

A coyote hunting in the Canadian Rockies.

Index